Today is a Cold Day

by Martha E. H. Rustad

raintree
a Capstone company — publishers for children

Raintree is an imprint of Capstone Global Library Limited, a company incorporated in England and Wales having its registered office at 264 Banbury Road, Oxford, OX2 7DY – Registered company number: 6695582

www.raintree.co.uk
myorders@raintree.co.uk

Edited by Marissa Kirkman
Designed by Charmaine Whitman and Peggie Carley
Picture research by Tracey Engel
Production by Katy LaVigne
Originated by Capstone Global Library
Printed and bound in China.

ISBN 978 1 4747 3877 4
20 19 18 17 16
10 9 8 7 6 5 4 3 2 1

British Library Cataloguing in Publication Data
A full catalogue record for this book is available from the British Library.

Acknowledgements
We would like to thank the following for permission to reproduce photographs: Glow Images: Bele Olmez, 16 (inset); Shutterstock: Aleksey Stemmer, 14, Aleksey Vanin, 6 (weather icons), Amy Nichole Harris, 18, Andrey Arkusha, 1, 10, iofoto, 8 (right), Juriah Mosin, 20, Kseniia Neverkovska, cover and interior design element, Lopolo, 8 (left), MANDY GODBEHEAR, 16, Nebojsa Markovic, 12, Ozerina Anna, cover and interior design element, Sergey Novikov, 4, Syda Productions, front cover, vinz89, 6 (thermometer)

Every effort has been made to contact copyright holders of material reproduced in this book. Any omissions will be rectified in subsequent printings if notice is given to the publisher.

Contents

What is the weather like?

Today is a cold day.

The temperature is low on

a cold day. Let's find out

how cold it is.

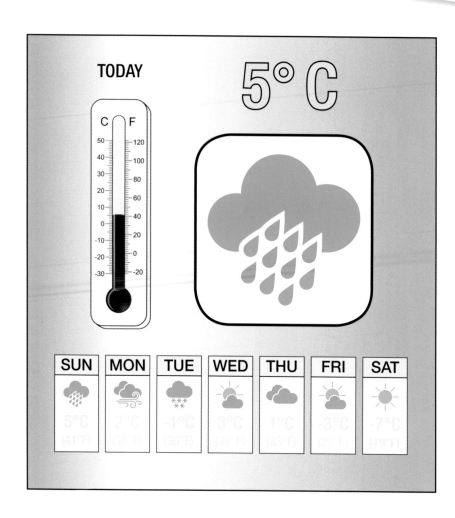

TODAY

5° C

SUN | MON | TUE | WED | THU | FRI | SAT

5°C | 2°C | -1°C | 3°C | 1°C | -3°C | -7°C
(41°F) | (36°F) | (30°F) | (38°F) | (33°F) | (27°F) | (19°F)

We can check the forecast.
It tells us what the weather
will be like. The numbers tell us
the temperature. The numbers
are smaller on cold days.

autumn

winter

The forecast also shows patterns.

Sometimes it is cold for

more than one day.

Autumn and winter have a lot

of cold days.

What do we see?

We see our breath on a cold day.
The air inside our bodies
is warm. The air outside is cold.
Our breath looks like a cloud
in the cold air.

We sometimes see rain on a cold day.

Rain turns into snow if

the temperature is cold enough.

Water freezes at 0 degrees Celsius

(32 degrees Fahrenheit).

We see frost on a
cold day. We also see ice
in puddles, rivers and lakes.
A whole lake can freeze
if the weather stays cold.

goosebumps

What do we do?

Brr! Cold air makes us shiver.

We have goosebumps. We wear

a coat to play outside

on a cold day.

Very, very cold weather

can cause frostbite.

We put on warm clothes.

A hat, scarf and gloves

cover our skin.

At the end of a cold day,

we eat warm soup for dinner.

Let's check the forecast for tomorrow!

Glossary

breath   the air you breathe in and out of your lungs

forecast   prediction of what the weather will be

frost   thin layer of ice crystals; frost forms outside in freezing weather

frostbite   frozen skin

goosebumps   tiny bumps that appear on people's skin when they are cold or frightened

pattern   several things that are repeated in the same way each time

shiver   to shake because of cold

temperature   the measured heat or cold of something; temperature is measured with a thermometer

Find out more

Books

Forecasts (Understanding Weather), Kristin Schuetz (Bellwether Media, 2016)

Weather in Winter (What Happens in Winter?), Jenny Fretland VanVoorst (Bullfrog Books, 2017)

What Can You See in Autumn? (Seasons), Sian Smith (Raintree, 2015)

Websites

scijinks.jpl.nasa.gov
Learn all about weather and forecasting with games and videos.

www.weatherwizkids.com/weather-temperature.htm
Learn all about temperature and find directions to perform your own temperature experiments.

youngmeteorologist.org
Play a game to learn all about weather and meteorology.

Index

Note to parents and teachers

The What is the Weather Today? series supports National Curriculum requirements for science related to weather. This book describes and illustrates a cold day. The images support early readers in understanding the text. The repetition of words and phrases helps early readers learn new words. This book also introduces early readers to subject-specific vocabulary words, which are defined in the Glossary section. Early readers may need assistance to read some words and to use the Contents, Glossary, Find out more and Index sections of the book.